W9-CIK-367

Jesus is Born!

Illustrated by Toni Goffe
Retold by LaVonne Neff

Tyndale House Publishers, Inc.

WHEATON · ILLINOIS

© 1994 Hunt & Thorpe
Illustrations © 1994 by Toni Goffe
All rights reserved

Published in the United States by
Tyndale House Publishers, Inc.
Wheaton, Illinois
Published in Great Britain by
Hunt & Thorpe

ISBN 0-8423-1864-X
Printed in Singapore

01 00 99 98 97 96 95 94
9 8 7 6 5 4 3 2 1

Contents

An Angel Visits Mary

Luke 1:26-38

There once was a girl named Mary who lived in a village called Nazareth. She was engaged to be married to a carpenter, Joseph. Mary was a good, sensible girl, and she never expected a visit from an angel.

But suddenly one day, without warning, the mighty angel Gabriel stood before her. "Greetings! The Lord is with you, " Gabriel said.

Mary stepped back in fear. "Don't be afraid, " said the angel. "You have found favor with God. You will have a son, and you will name him Jesus. He will be King forever."

"How can this be?" Mary asked. "I am a virgin."

Gabriel answered, "The Holy Spirit will make this happen. That is why your child will be called the Son of God."

Mary knew that God had sent the angel to her.

"I am the Lord's servant," she said. "Let it be to me as you have said."

Mary Visits Elizabeth

Luke 1:39-56

The angel Gabriel brought Mary good news about her cousin Elizabeth. Elizabeth had no children, and now she was old. "Soon Elizabeth will have a son, " Gabriel said. "With God, nothing is impossible. "

Mary quickly left for Elizabeth's house. When she arrived, she did not have to tell her cousin what had happened. Elizabeth, filled with the Holy Spirit, already knew. "You are blessed among women, and blessed is the child you will bear," Elizabeth said. "I am honored that the mother of my Lord should visit me!"

Mary said, "My spirit rejoices in God, my Savior. From now on, everyone will call me blessed, for God has done great things for me. He brings down the proud, and he lifts up the humble. He fills the hungry with good things, and he sends the rich away empty.

In his mercy, he helps his people."

Mary stayed with Elizabeth for three months.

An Angel Speaks to Joseph

Matthew 1:18-25

When Mary returned from Elizabeth's house, she talked to Joseph. She told him about Gabriel's visit. She told him about Elizabeth's baby. And she told him that she also was going to have a baby.

Joseph did not know what to do. He did not want to marry her if she was having someone else's baby. But he did not want to shame her either. Maybe he could break up with her quietly.

One night an angel came to Joseph in a dream. "Don't be afraid to take Mary as your wife," the angel said. "Her baby is from the Holy Spirit. She will give birth to a son, and you will name him Jesus. He will save his people from their sins."

When Joseph woke up, he obeyed the angel. He brought Mary to his home to be his wife. Together, Joseph and Mary waited for the promised baby.

No Room in the Inn

Luke 2:1-5

In those days, the emperor decided to count all the people he ruled. He ordered everyone to return to his or her hometown to be counted. Joseph and Mary had to travel to Bethlehem.

It took nearly a week to go from Nazareth to Bethlehem. When Joseph and Mary finally arrived, they saw people everywhere. Some were camping in the town square. Others had stopped by the side of the road.

"The inn is full," someone told them.

Mary was tired. She knew it was time for her baby to be born.

Joseph went up to the inn and knocked on the door. He told the innkeeper that Mary was going to have a baby.

"I'm sorry," said the innkeeper, "but we don't have any rooms. We don't even have any quiet corners where she could lie down."

"What will we do?" asked Mary.

"I don't know," said Joseph.

Jesus Is Born!

Luke 2:6-7

Behind the inn, there was a cave; and inside the cave, there was a stable where travelers kept their animals. The stable-cave was quiet, warm, and dark.

"Let's go into the stable," Joseph said. "We can make a bed on the straw. It's better than sleeping outside."

During the night, Mary's baby was born. Mary wrapped him in long strips of cloth to keep him warm. She made a bed for him in a manger full of straw.

Mary remembered Gabriel's words: "You will have a son, and … he will be King forever." She wondered what the angel meant.

Why would a king be born in a stable instead of a fine house?

Why would a king sleep on scratchy straw in a feeding trough instead of on satin cushions in a cradle?

Why would a king's birth be greeted only by donkeys and chickens and little stray cats?

Angels Sing to the Shepherds

Luke 2:8-15

That night in the fields outside Bethlehem, some sleepy shepherds were watching their flocks of sheep. Suddenly an angel appeared before them, and dazzling light shone all around. The shepherds were terrified.

"Don't be afraid, " said the angel. "I bring you good news of great joy for all people. Today in Bethlehem, your Savior has been born. This is how you will know him: you will find a baby wrapped in strips of cloth, lying in a manger."

All at once, the sky was full of angels singing praises to God:

"Glory to God in the highest, and peace on earth to those with whom he is pleased!"

Then, as quickly as they had come, the angels disappeared. Once again the sky was dark. But the shepherds were wide awake.

"Let's go to Bethlehem," they said to each other. "Let's see this baby that God has told us about."

The Shepherds Visit the Baby

Luke 2:16-20

Mary and Joseph were resting in the stable when they heard footsteps and loud talking. "This must be the place, " someone said. "At least it has a manger."

Several rough-looking men and boys came through the doorway. "There he is," one said, pointing at the newborn baby.

" 'A baby, wrapped in strips of cloth, lying in a manger.' That's what the angel told us," said another.

"This is the Savior," said a young shepherd boy. "This is the Lord."

The men and boys knelt down before the baby.

Then the shepherds nodded to Mary and Joseph and ran out of the stable. Mary could hear them shouting, "Glory to God in the highest!" She could hear them telling everyone they met that the Savior was born.

The Savior, Mary thought. *The Lord. The King. The Son of God. … Who is this child of mine?*

Mary and Joseph Bring Jesus to the Temple

Luke 2:21-38

Mary and Joseph named the baby Jesus, just as the angel had told them to do. They took Baby Jesus to the temple to present him to the Lord.

Near the temple lived an old man named Simeon. The Holy Spirit had told Simeon he would not die until he saw the Savior. One day, the Holy Spirit told Simeon to go to the temple. When he arrived, he saw Mary and Joseph and Jesus.

Simeon took Baby Jesus in his arms. He said, "Lord, now I can die in peace, for I have seen your Savior, a light for the whole world."

At the temple lived a very old woman named Anna. Anna was a prophet. When she saw Baby Jesus, she gave thanks to God. Then she began to tell people that the Savior was born.

Mary and Joseph were amazed at what people were saying about Jesus.

The Wise Men Follow a Star
Matthew 2:1-6

In a distant, eastern land lived some wise men. They studied holy books, and they knew that a mighty King would soon be born. They studied the sky, and one night they saw a new star.

"The King is born," they said. "Let us go worship him."

The wise men gathered together much food and water and many rich gifts. They followed the star for many months. They passed through wide, empty deserts. They climbed high mountains. They crossed deep rivers.

When they got to Jerusalem, the wise men stopped. They asked everyone, "Where is the newborn King?"

In Jerusalem, the priests and scholars had also been studying the Scriptures. "The Bible says that Israel's ruler will come from Bethlehem," they said.

Bethlehem was only a few miles from Jerusalem. The wise men got ready to see the new King.

The Wise Men Visit Jesus

Matthew 2:9-11

That evening the wise men looked at the sky. Once again they saw the star. It was shining over Bethlehem.

They left immediately for the little town. Now the star shone directly over a house. Could this be where the new King lived? It did not look like a palace.

The wise men went up to the door and knocked. Inside they found the baby Jesus with Mary, his mother. The wise men bowed down and worshiped the little King. Then they gave him the gifts they had brought.

They gave him gold, because he was a King who would rule the world.

They gave him incense, because he was a Priest who would bring people to God.

And they gave him myrrh, because he would die to save people from sin.

When the wise men left the house, they were full of joy. They had seen the Savior of the world.